weird but true!

BIRTHDAYS

weird but true!

BIRTHDAYS

300 FUN-TASTIC FACTS TO CELEBRATE

NATIONAL GEOGRAPHIC
WASHINGTON, D.C.

IF 23 PEOPLE

GATHER IN A GROUP, THERE'S ABOUT A

50 PERCENT CHANCE

THAT AT LEAST TWO OF THEM WILL SHARE THE

SAME BIRTHDAY.

THE SULTAN OF BRUNEI HAD ONE OF THE WORLD'S **MOST EXPENSIVE BIRTHDAY PARTIES:** A $25 MILLION BASH WITH A PERFORMANCE BY **MICHAEL JACKSON.**

A JAPANESE ARTIST SCULPTS **LIFELIKE** ANIMALS, INCLUDING RABBITS, SLOTHS, AND BUTTERFLIES, USING NOTHING BUT **BALLOONS.**

THE TOWN OF **TWINSBURG, OHIO, U.S.A.,** HOSTS AN ANNUAL **TWINS DAYS FESTIVAL,** WHICH INCLUDES A "DOUBLE TAKE" PARADE.

ON SATURN AND JUPITER, IT CAN

RAIN
APRIL'S BIRTHSTONE:

DIAMONDS.

SOME COMPANIES MAKE **FAKE DINOSAUR EGGS** THAT CAN BE CRACKED OPEN TO REVEAL **BIRTHDAY INVITATIONS.**

In the United States, SEPTEMBER 9 is the most common birthday.

And the LEAST COMMON birthday is December 25.

According to a survey, about **70 percent** of pet owners add their **pet's name** when signing **birthday cards.**

HAPPY BIRTHDAY!

xoxo,
Jake &
Sparky 🐾

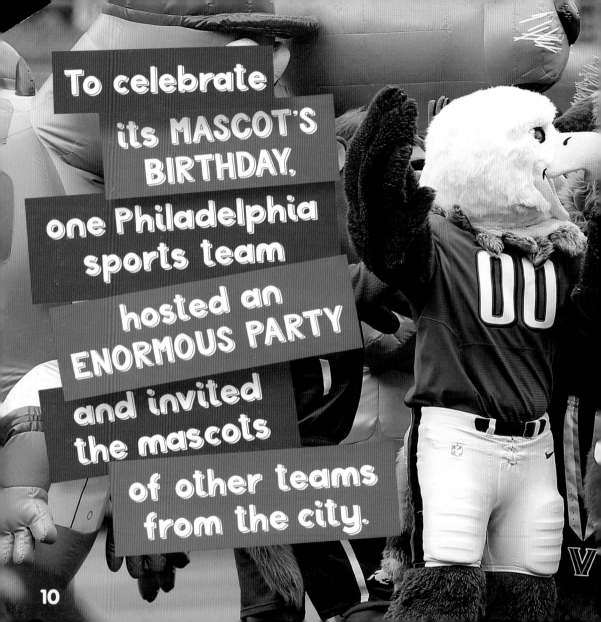

To celebrate its MASCOT'S BIRTHDAY, one Philadelphia sports team hosted an ENORMOUS PARTY and invited the mascots of other teams from the city.

Baseball player Babe Ruth **FOUND OUT HIS BIRTHDAY WAS FEBRUARY 6, 1895,** instead of February 7, 1894, but he continued to celebrate the wrong birthday.

One man popped

78 confetti-filled party poppers

in one minute.

Zodiac signs
were created based on the
STAR CONSTELLATIONS
that the sun appears to
"MOVE THROUGH"
as the Earth orbits
around it in a year.

Poop-themed party invitations and favors are available for purchase.

You can send someone a birthday gift box with a cake, photographs, and **FAKE BUTTERFLIES** that fly out when it's opened.

14

One variety of ROSE, June's birth flower, sold for **$15.8 MILLION** in 2006.

DECEMBER'S BIRTH FLOWER

Legend says that it's **BAD LUCK** to cut down a holly tree.

SOME SPECIES OF **CICADA** STAY UNDERGROUND UNTIL THEIR 17TH BIRTHDAY, WHEN **BILLIONS SURFACE** TO LOOK FOR A MATE.

A FAMOUS NEW YORK CITY STATUE OF A BULL, **THE SYMBOL OF TAURUS,** WEIGHS MORE THAN **THREE REAL BULLS,** AT 7,000 POUNDS (3,175 KG).

YOU CAN BUY EDIBLE BIRTHDAY CANDLES.

A HIGH SCHOOL IN ILLINOIS, U.S.A., HAD THE MOST **TWIN** PAIRS IN THE SAME CLASS: 44.

Sapphires, September's birthstone, were once thought to be an antidote to **POISON.**

17

More than **2,000 years ago,** the Babylonians created Western astrology, a system they believed could **predict someone's future** based on **where the stars were** at the time of that person's birth.

A bakery in Boston, Massachusetts, U.S.A., created a banana-cream-filled, chocolate-and-caramel-frosted

DOUGHNUT

to celebrate Curious George's 75th birthday.

A tree in California, U.S.A., has had almost **5,000** **birthdays.**

In Australia, **sprinkles** are called **"hundreds and thousands."**

ONE FAMILY HAD **FIVE CHILDREN** BORN IN DIFFERENT YEARS WHO ALL SHARED THE **SAME BIRTHDAY.**

ONE PIG, AN ANIMAL FOUND IN THE CHINESE ZODIAC, HAS A SOCIAL MEDIA ACCOUNT WHERE SHE DRESSED UP IN A MERMAID TAIL AS A **"MERPIG."**

A manta ray found off the Great Barrier Reef was **BORN PINK—** the world's only known ray of that color.

M&M'S created the **WORLD'S LARGEST PIÑATA:** a 47-foot (14.32-m)-high, 68.6-foot (20.9-m)-long orange M&M standing on a birthday cake.

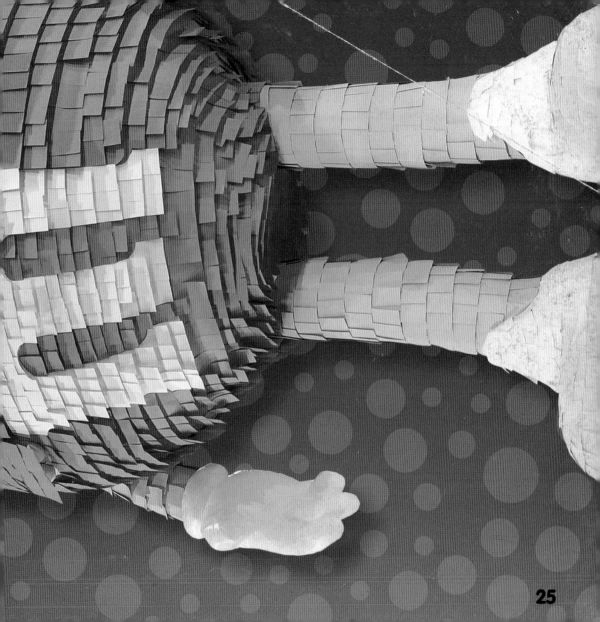

IN 2017, ONE MAN RECEIVED **32,207 VIDEOS** CONTAINING BIRTHDAY GREETINGS— A WORLD RECORD.

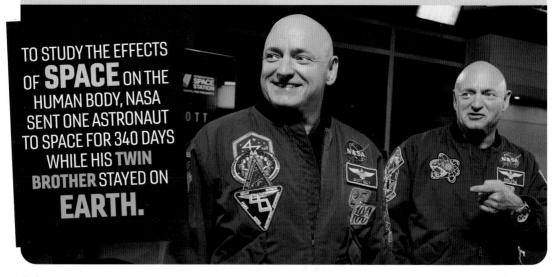

TO STUDY THE EFFECTS OF **SPACE** ON THE HUMAN BODY, NASA SENT ONE ASTRONAUT TO SPACE FOR 340 DAYS WHILE HIS **TWIN BROTHER** STAYED ON **EARTH.**

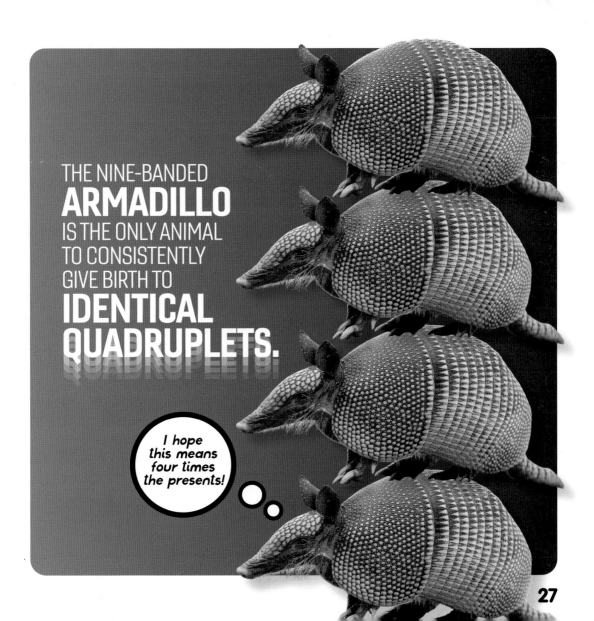

THE NINE-BANDED **ARMADILLO** IS THE ONLY ANIMAL TO CONSISTENTLY GIVE BIRTH TO **IDENTICAL QUADRUPLETS.**

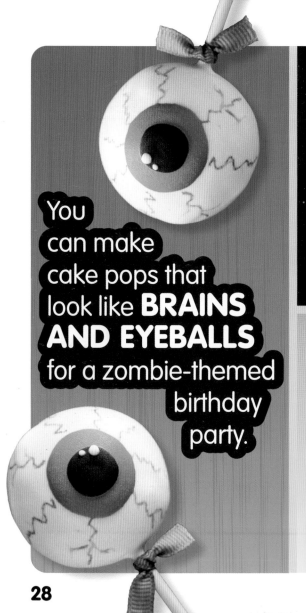

You can make cake pops that look like **BRAINS AND EYEBALLS** for a zombie-themed birthday party.

Scientists used measurements gathered by **NASA'S KEPLER SPACECRAFT** to determine the **AGE OF STARS.**

According to astrological legend about the Western zodiac, people born under **Capricorn, Taurus,** and **Virgo** are

HARD WORKERS

because they are influenced by the **Earth** element.

Rabbits, an animal found in the Chinese zodiac, CAN'T VOMIT.

AUSTRALIA GIFTED ONE BRITISH PRINCE AN UNUSUAL PRESENT: A BABY CROCODILE THAT HATCHED ON THE SAME DAY A ROYAL PREGNANCY WAS ANNOUNCED.

A woman in Italy once used her feet to light **11** birthday candles **IN UNDER ONE MINUTE.**

Cupcakes got their name from a recipe that appeared in an American cookbook in 1828 that measured ingredients in drinking **cups.**

National Winnie the Pooh Day celebrates author A. A. Milne's birthday on January 18.

A WEBCAM
was added to the Statue of Liberty's
TORCH
on its 125th birthday, live-streaming
views of New York Harbor
and the city's skyline.

ACCORDING TO BELIEFS FROM ANCIENT ASTROLOGY, PEOPLE BORN ON MONDAYS ARE **INFLUENCED BY THE MOON,** MAKING THEM **KIND AND CARING.**

THE CLOTHING USED TO DRESS KING TUTANKHAMUN IN HIS TOMB WAS PARTLY MADE FROM THE **POPPY PLANT,** AUGUST'S BIRTH FLOWER.

A bakery in Seattle, Washington, U.S.A., created a cupcake topped with **A LOLLIPOP,** cookies, and doughnut holes for its 10th birthday.

BOYS born in NOVEMBER, DECEMBER, or JANUARY are more likely to be LEFT-HANDED, a study found.

The Aztec used **MARIGOLDS,** October's birth flower, to cure hiccups.

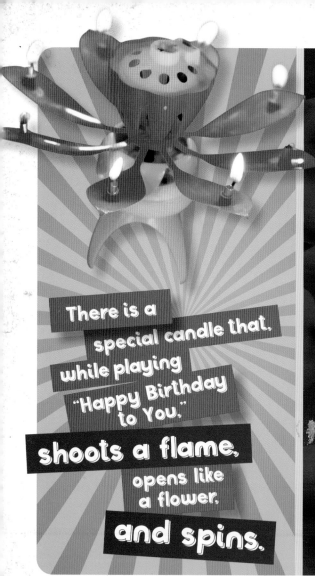

There is a special candle that, while playing "Happy Birthday to You," shoots a flame, opens like a flower, and spins.

Scientists can ESTIMATE someone's age by analyzing just one drop of BLOOD.

QUEEN ELIZABETH HAS

TWO BIRTHDAYS:

HER ACTUAL BIRTHDAY AND AN

OFFICIAL ONE

SCHEDULED TO BE CELEBRATED DURING GOOD WEATHER.

IN 2012, U.S. PRESIDENT BARACK OBAMA'S DOG BO CELEBRATED HIS FOURTH BIRTHDAY WITH BONE-SHAPED **TREATS** AND A PUP PLAYDATE AT THE **WHITE HOUSE.**

Most people **DON'T REMEMBER** their first three years of life.

As soon as they're born, giant Pacific octopuses can change their color at will to hide from predators.

MORE THAN A QUARTER OF PEOPLE BORN IN DECEMBER SAY THAT THEIR **BIRTHDAY PRESENTS** ARE **WRAPPED** IN **CHRISTMAS PAPER.**

Two people from the United Kingdom **SET A RECORD by** popping 51 party poppers in **30 SECONDS.**

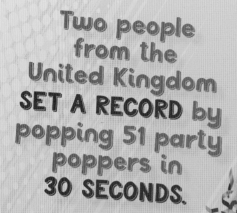

POLAND once sent the United States a **BIRTHDAY CARD** signed by more than **FIVE MILLION PEOPLE** that was about 30,000 pages long.

There is a species of crab, Cancer's symbol, that uses tiny pieces of **stinging sea anemone** to fight off predators.

IN HONOR OF GEORGE WASHINGTON'S BIRTHDAY, U.S. PRESIDENT ANDREW JACKSON INVITED THE PUBLIC TO THE WHITE HOUSE, WHERE 10,000 GUESTS DINED ON A NEARLY **1,400-POUND** (635-KG) HUNK OF CHEESE.

Astrological tradition holds that **Cancer, Scorpio,** and **Pisces** are **water** signs in the Western zodiac, supposedly making people with those signs **emotional and creative.**

ABOUT 14 TIMES MORE *BACTERIA* IS FOUND ON CAKE AFTER SOMEONE *BLOWS OUT THEIR BIRTHDAY CANDLES.*

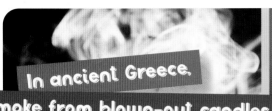

In ancient Greece, smoke from blown-out candles was said to carry wishes to the gods.

SpaceX launched a **ROCKET** with chocolate, vanilla, and birthday-cake-flavored ice cream on board for astronauts on the **INTERNATIONAL SPACE STATION.**

IN 1969, ASTRONAUT **NEIL ARMSTRONG** CELEBRATED HIS 39TH BIRTHDAY IN QUARANTINE TO MAKE SURE THE APOLLO 11 CREW HADN'T BROUGHT BACK ANY **"MOON BUGS."**

One study found that **DOGS,** an animal included in the Chinese zodiac, prefer humans' "baby talk" to their regular speech.

47

TO CELEBRATE HIS **75TH, 80TH, 85TH, AND 90TH** BIRTHDAYS, U.S. PRESIDENT GEORGE H. W. BUSH WENT **SKYDIVING.**

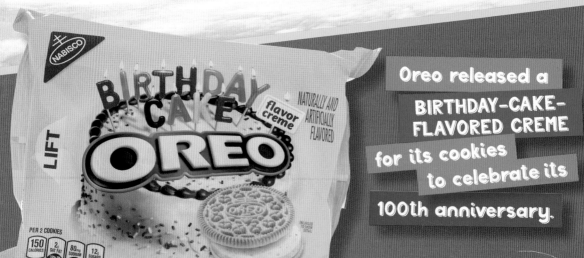

Oreo released a BIRTHDAY-CAKE-FLAVORED CREME for its cookies to celebrate its 100th anniversary.

Madagascar's Labord

CHAMELEON

**dies before its first birthday
when the region's dry season begins.**

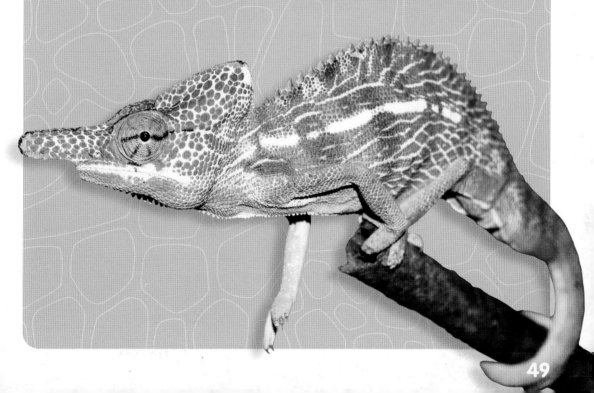

Wishing you a Happy BIRTHDAY

ON EACH BIRTHDAY, YOU ARE **31,536,000 SECONDS** OLDER THAN YOU WERE ON YOUR LAST BIRTHDAY.

Two U.S. women have been sending each other the **SAME BIRTHDAY CARD** since 1944!

HIP-HOP MUSIC WAS "BORN" AT A BIRTHDAY PARTY IN NEW YORK CITY IN 1973.

You likely share your birthday with about **20.8 MILLION PEOPLE** around the globe.

Boys in ancient Rome were given **MEDALLIONS** meant to ward off evil, which they wore until they reached adulthood.

Foiled again!

A WOMAN BORN IN TEXAS, U.S.A., HAS A FIRST NAME THAT'S MORE THAN **1,000 LETTERS LONG.**

MVD CALIFORNIA

DRIVER LICENSE

1995

TO FIT HER NAME, THE BIRTH CERTIFICATE NEEDED TO BE ALMOST TWICE AS LONG AS USUAL.

According to legends from astrology, people **born on Sundays** are influenced by **the sun,** making them

creative
and bold.

To celebrate their **40th birthday,** one restaurant chain offered **a year of free burgers** to anyone who got a **permanent tattoo** of their logo.

The world's largest **connect-the-dots** picture, of the **beloved character the BFG,** was created to honor author **Roald Dahl's 100th birthday.**

People once believed that EMERALDS, May's birthstone, could MELT SNAKES' EYES.

ACCORDING TO SUPERSTITION, YOUR CHINESE ZODIAC YEAR, WHICH OCCURS EVERY 12 YEARS AFTER YOUR BIRTH,

MAY BRING BAD LUCK,

WHICH YOU CAN COUNTERACT BY

WEARING RED.

In 2010, visitors at **Yosemite National Park** in California, U.S.A., saw the **International Space Station** as it flew over to celebrate the park's 120th birthday.

One woman owns the **world's largest confetti collection:** nearly **1,500 shapes.**

In addition to fish, **FEET** also represent the astrological sign Pisces.

In 1991, 850 CLOWNS met up in England,

setting the record for the LARGEST GATHERING of professional clowns.

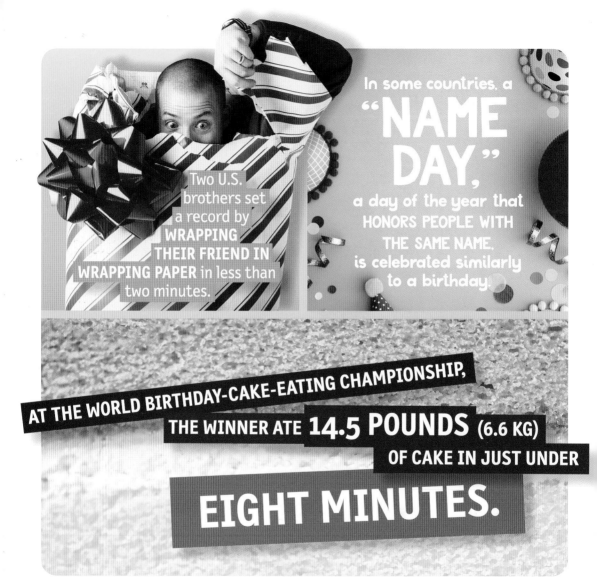

Two U.S. brothers set a record by **WRAPPING THEIR FRIEND IN WRAPPING PAPER** in less than two minutes.

In some countries, a "**NAME DAY**," a day of the year that HONORS PEOPLE WITH THE SAME NAME, is celebrated similarly to a birthday.

AT THE WORLD BIRTHDAY-CAKE-EATING CHAMPIONSHIP, THE WINNER ATE **14.5 POUNDS** (6.6 KG) OF CAKE IN JUST UNDER **EIGHT MINUTES.**

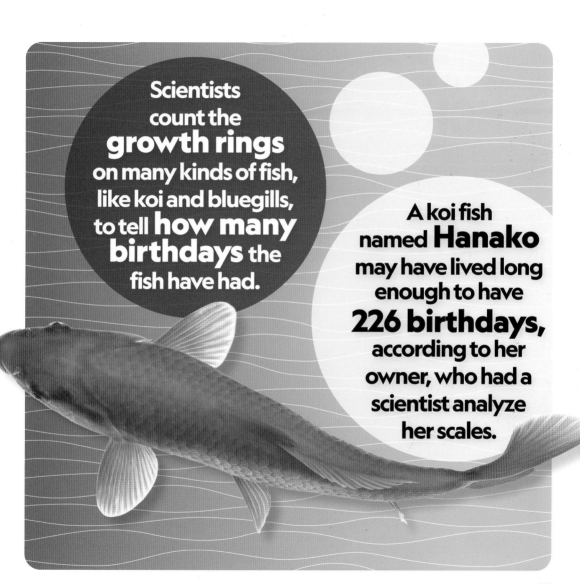

Scientists count the **growth rings** on many kinds of fish, like koi and bluegills, to tell **how many birthdays** the fish have had.

A koi fish named **Hanako** may have lived long enough to have **226 birthdays,** according to her owner, who had a scientist analyze her scales.

At the
ENCHANTED CAVE
in Australia,
visitors can see a geode
that is larger than an

ELEPHANT

and full
of amethyst,

February's
birthstone.

IN ANCIENT **ROME**, SPECIAL CAKES MADE WITH FLOUR, OLIVE OIL, HONEY, AND GRATED CHEESE WERE GIVEN TO THOSE CELEBRATING THEIR 50TH BIRTHDAY.

CALVIN COOLIDGE is the only U.S. president **BORN ON THE FOURTH OF JULY,** the birthday of the **UNITED STATES.**

One baker made a realistic cake that looked like a

GIANT HISSING COCKROACH

... and stuffed it with cream filling!

SKATEBOARDING WAS "BORN" IN THE 1940s OR 1950s WHEN **SURFERS** CREATED SOMETHING TO RIDE WHEN THE WAVES WERE FLAT.

At 7,475 feet (2,278.5 m), one necklace made of JUNE'S BIRTHSTONE, PEARLS, is almost three times as long as the WORLD'S TALLEST BUILDING.

Child actor **Shirley Temple** received more than **135,000 PRESENTS** for her eighth birthday.

SOME COMPANIES USE JANUARY'S BIRTHSTONE, **GARNET,** TO MAKE **SANDPAPER.**

At the **NATIONAL MUSEUM OF AMERICAN HISTORY** in Washington, D.C., you can see pieces of cake from U.S. president **FRANKLIN D. ROOSEVELT'S** 1934 birthday party.

A music company once **owned the rights** to "Happy Birthday to You" and collected about **$2 million** annually from its use in TV and film.

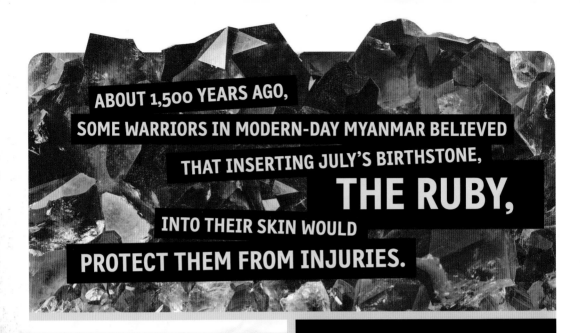

ABOUT 1,500 YEARS AGO, SOME WARRIORS IN MODERN-DAY MYANMAR BELIEVED THAT INSERTING JULY'S BIRTHSTONE, **THE RUBY,** INTO THEIR SKIN WOULD PROTECT THEM FROM INJURIES.

You can buy BIRTHDAY-CAKE-SCENTED pencils.

A celebrity once gave her husband **A TRIP TO SPACE** for his birthday.

FOR HIS 63RD BIRTHDAY, U.S. PRESIDENT HARRY TRUMAN WAS GIVEN HIS OWN **BOWLING ALLEY** IN THE WHITE HOUSE.

A TINY ISLAND OFF BRAZIL IS
SWARMING
WITH UP TO
4,000 SNAKES,
A CHINESE ZODIAC ANIMAL.

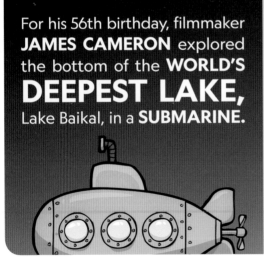

For his 56th birthday, filmmaker **JAMES CAMERON** explored the bottom of the **WORLD'S DEEPEST LAKE,** Lake Baikal, in a **SUBMARINE.**

SOME SPECIES OF **MAYFLY** ARE BORN AND THEN DIE WITHIN **TWO DAYS.**

BASKETBALL STARS LEBRON JAMES AND STEPHEN CURRY **WERE BORN IN THE SAME HOSPITAL.**

Scientists spotted **GIANT PILLARS OF GAS** on the sun that they described as looking like **CANDLES** on a birthday cake.

CALLED THE **"CROWN" YEARS,** AGES 5, 10, 15, 20, AND 21 ARE CELEBRATED IN HOLLAND WITH AN **ESPECIALLY BIG GIFT.**

IN GUIZHOU, CHINA, A **WATERFALL** EMERGES FROM THE HEAD OF AN **ENORMOUS** STATUE OF A **GOLDEN DRAGON,** AN ANIMAL IN THE CHINESE ZODIAC.

ONE BOY'S **SIXTH BIRTHDAY CAKE** COULD **TRANSFORM** FROM A **TRUCK** INTO A **TALKING ROBOT.**

MORE THAN 500 MUSICIANS IN
SWITZERLAND CELEBRATED THE

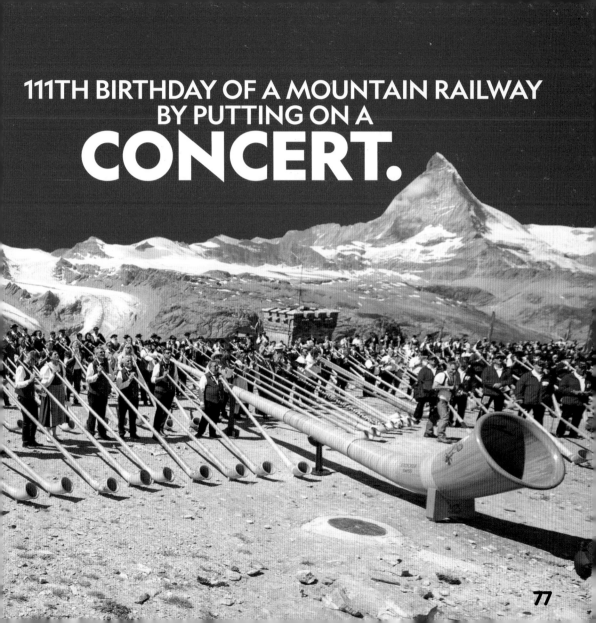

111TH BIRTHDAY OF A MOUNTAIN RAILWAY BY PUTTING ON A **CONCERT.**

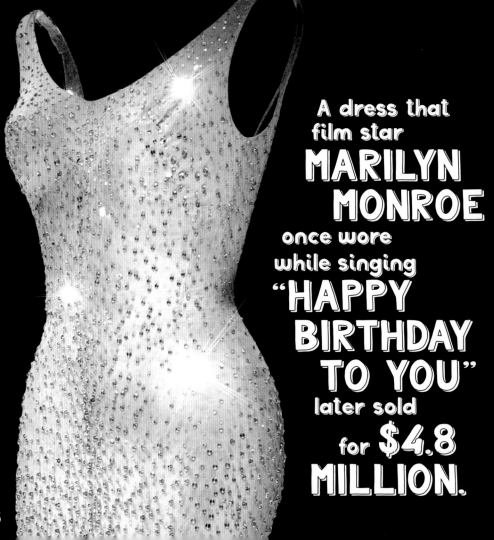

A dress that film star **MARILYN MONROE** once wore while singing **"HAPPY BIRTHDAY TO YOU"** later sold for **$4.8 MILLION.**

THE EIFFEL TOWER was built as a **TEMPORARY ENTRYWAY** to a world's fair held in Paris in 1889, which celebrated the **100TH BIRTHDAY OF THE FRENCH REVOLUTION.**

IN WALES, U.K., LEGEND HOLDS THAT IF YOU SPOT THE SEASON'S **FIRST DAFFODIL,** MARCH'S BIRTH FLOWER, THE NEXT YEAR WILL BRING **WEALTH.**

THERE HAVE BEEN MORE **U.S. PRESIDENTS** BORN UNDER **SCORPIO** THAN ANY OTHER SIGN.

BASKETBALL LEGEND **SHAQUILLE O'NEAL** GAVE AWAY OREO TREATS FROM THE **"SNACK SHAQ"** TO CELEBRATE HIS SHARED MARCH 6 BIRTHDAY WITH **THE OREO COOKIE.**

FOUR OF THE FIVE AQUARIUS PRESIDENTS **DIED** WHILE IN OFFICE, AND THE FIFTH WAS NEARLY **ASSASSINATED.**

The earliest documented twins, Gemini's symbol, lived more than **30,000 years ago.**

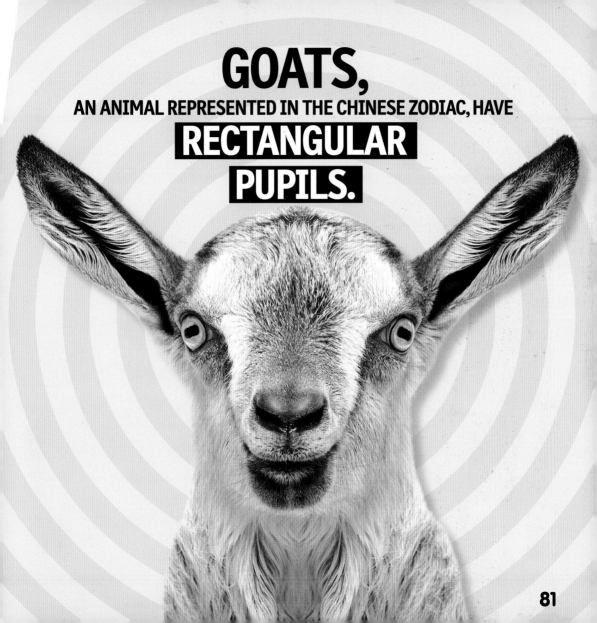

GOATS,

AN ANIMAL REPRESENTED IN THE CHINESE ZODIAC, HAVE

RECTANGULAR
PUPILS.

Archaeologists discovered **DINOSAUR BONES** that, over 100 million years, had turned into October's birthstone,

OPAL.

PLACES ON THE CHINESE ZODIAC AFTER WINNING A *RACE.*

I'm back!

A BEETLE that Charles Darwin collected in 1832 was **REDISCOVERED** in 2014 and **DECLARED A NEW SPECIES** on his 205th birthday.

In late 18th-century Germany, **A CHILD AWOKE** on their birthday to a cake topped with lit candles that were **CONTINUALLY REPLACED** so they would burn until after dinner.

AT ONE PARTY, A **LIFE-SIZE CHOCOLATE CAR** THAT COST MORE THAN **$20,000** WAS BROKEN INTO PIECES AND GIVEN TO GUESTS AS **PARTY FAVORS.**

FESTIVAL DEL CIOCCOLATO

There is a type of MONKEY, a Chinese zodiac animal, with a BLUE FACE.

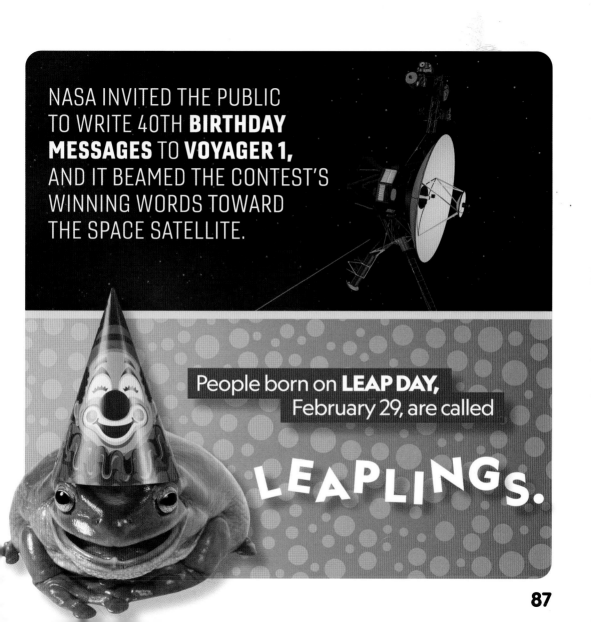

NASA INVITED THE PUBLIC TO WRITE 40TH **BIRTHDAY MESSAGES** TO **VOYAGER 1,** AND IT BEAMED THE CONTEST'S WINNING WORDS TOWARD THE SPACE SATELLITE.

People born on **LEAP DAY,** February 29, are called

LEAPLINGS.

YOU CAN BUY DECORATIONS, INVITATIONS, BALLOONS, AND CAKE TOPPERS FOR A **GARBAGE-TRUCK-THEMED** BIRTHDAY PARTY.

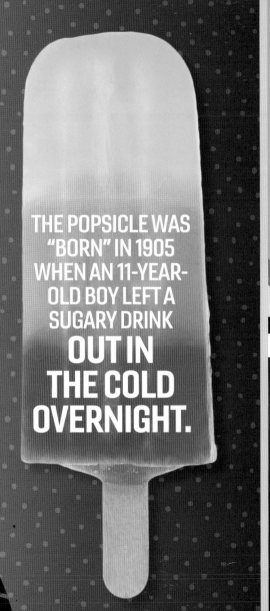

THE POPSICLE WAS "BORN" IN 1905 WHEN AN 11-YEAR-OLD BOY LEFT A SUGARY DRINK **OUT IN THE COLD OVERNIGHT.**

To mark the 50th birthday of **HOT WHEELS,** fans could buy a **LIFE-SIZE VERSION** of its first toy car, a 1968 Camaro.

The odds of being born in the first minute of a new year and getting **STRUCK BY LIGHTNING** are about the same.

On the **30th birthday** of the **Hubble Space Telescope,** NASA released an image of the **"COSMIC REEF,"** a star nursery resembling a **coral reef.**

ROCK STAR **PAUL MCCARTNEY'S** ORIGINAL **BIRTH CERTIFICATE** WAS ONCE AUCTIONED FOR MORE THAN

$70,000.

A MAGIC TRICK FROM THE EARLY 1800'S— CALLED PEPPER'S GHOST— IS USED TO MAKE *DANCING GHOSTS* APPEAR AT A BIRTHDAY PARTY IN *DISNEY'S HAUNTED MANSION ATTRACTION.*

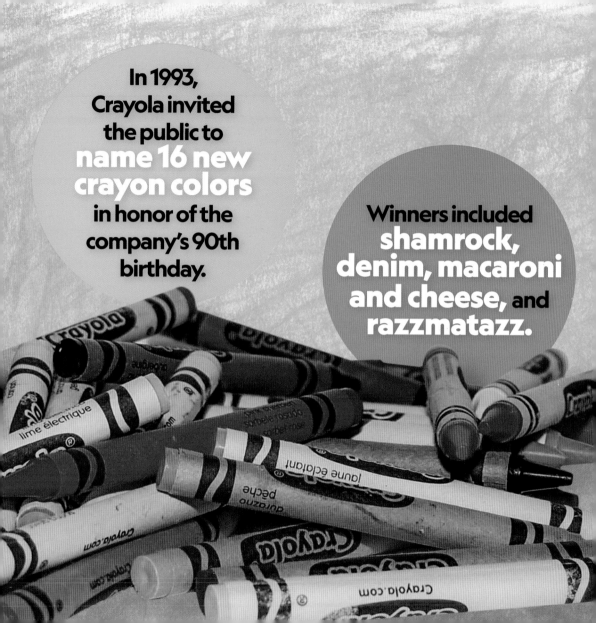

In 1993, Crayola invited the public to **name 16 new crayon colors** in honor of the company's 90th birthday.

Winners included **shamrock, denim, macaroni and cheese,** and **razzmatazz.**

MICKEY MOUSE'S **BIRTHDAY,** NOVEMBER 18, IS THE DAY HIS FIRST CARTOON **PREMIERED.**

One family set a record for having **THREE CONSECUTIVE GENERATIONS** born on

LEAP DAY.

PEOPLE WHOSE **AGE ENDS IN A 9** ARE MORE LIKELY TO SIGN UP TO **RUN A MARATHON,** A STUDY FOUND.

PERIDOT, AUGUST'S BIRTHSTONE, CAN BE FOUND IN **METEORITES.**

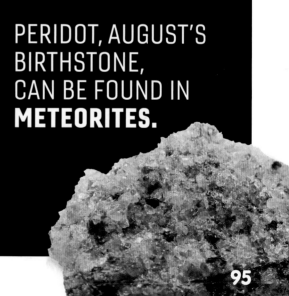

The Burj Khalifa in **DUBAI**, United Arab Emirates, the world's tallest building at the time, was lit up with the colors of **INDIA'S FLAG** to celebrate the birthday of the country's constitution.

THE RECORD FOR
THE **MOST DIAMONDS**,
APRIL'S BIRTHSTONE,
ON ONE RING IS

12,638.

IN 2019, BIG BIRD FLIPPED THE
CEREMONIAL SWITCH THAT LIT
THE **EMPIRE STATE BUILDING**
GREEN AND YELLOW TO
CELEBRATE *SESAME STREET'S*
50TH BIRTHDAY.

THE WORLD RECORD FOR THE
MOST CANDLES ON ONE BIRTHDAY CAKE IS **72,585.**

IT TOOK **60 BLOWTORCHES** TO LIGHT THEM.

For your birthday, you can rent a **giant inflatable slide** that looks like an octopus attacking a ship.

According to traditional beliefs about the Western zodiac, **Aries, Leo,** and **Sagittarius** signs are very **enthusiastic** because they are influenced by **fire.**

THE WORLD'S MOST EXPENSIVE

BIRTHDAY CAKE

WAS A $75 MILLION FASHION-SHOW-THEMED TREAT STUDDED WITH 4,000 DIAMONDS.

For hundreds of years, newborn babies were gifted CORAL RATTLES, which were believed to protect them from EVIL AND ILLNESS.

A woman in Italy trained her dog to be able to untie ribbon bows.

A horse, one of the animals of the Chinese zodiac, can walk within an hour or two of being born.

ONE MAJOR LEAGUE BASEBALL PLAYER SCORED A **HOME RUN** ON HIS BIRTHDAY **FOUR YEARS** IN A ROW.

ONE COMPANY OFFERS THE OPTION OF **MAILING SOMEONE A POTATO WITH THEIR FACE ON IT,** AS A **BIRTHDAY PRANK.**

Lion cubs in a pride often have birthdays around the same time so their moms can care for all the cubs together.

TRICK CANDLES, *WHICH RELIGHT AFTER THEY'RE BLOWN OUT, ARE BANNED IN CANADA.*

The sun actually "moves through" a **13TH ZODIAC SIGN** called **OPHIUCHUS,** shaped like a person holding a snake.

When creating the zodiac, the Babylonians left out **OPHIUCHUS** because they preferred to have **12 SIGNS FOR 12 MONTHS.**

Sailors once believed that **aquamarine,** March's birthstone, would bring them **good luck at sea.**

To celebrate the 20th birthday of the **London Eye Ferris wheel,** 20 of its pods were **specially decorated** inside, including one as a **kids birthday party** with face-painting.

"DAISY" COMES FROM WORDS THAT MEAN **"DAY'S EYE"** BECAUSE THE PETALS OF APRIL'S BIRTH FLOWER **CLOSE AT NIGHT** AND OPEN AT DAWN.

For the 375th birthday of Montreal, Canada, the city added lights to one of its bridges, which flash different colors to reflect the city's **"mood."**

I'm cute ... and deadly!

SOME SCIENTISTS THINK THAT WHEN THEY HATCH, **BABY PUFFERFISH** ARE COVERED IN THEIR MOTHER'S **POISON.**

JOHN ADAMS and **THOMAS JEFFERSON** both died on July 4, 1826—the 50th birthday of the adoption of the **DECLARATION OF INDEPENDENCE.**

In the Western zodiac, Libra, Gemini, and Aquarius are

AIR SIGNS,

which astrological lore says makes them logical and adventurous.

IN CONGRESS, JULY 4, 1776.

The unanimous Declaration of the thirteen united States of America.

YOU CAN BUY SOMEONE A **BOOK THAT CONTAINS NEWSPAPERS** PUBLISHED FROM THEIR **DATE OF BIRTH** AND EVERY BIRTHDAY AFTER.

Crumbs can be **DANGEROUS** in space, so one astronaut celebrated his birthday with an **INFLATABLE CAKE.**

In the Harry Potter series, Fred and George Weasley, characters known for their **PRACTICAL JOKES,** were born on **APRIL FOOLS' DAY.**

ACCORDING TO SOME ANCIENT BELIEFS, **EVIL SPIRITS** VISITED PEOPLE ON THEIR BIRTHDAY, SO FRIENDS GATHERED TO **MAKE NOISE** AND SCARE THEM AWAY.

SINCE 1917, U.K. monarchs have sent birthday greetings to those celebrating their **100TH BIRTHDAY.**

IN 2012, **228 PEOPLE** BORN ON JULY 4 GATHERED ON THEIR BIRTHDAY IN APELDOORN, NETHERLANDS, TO **BREAK A WORLD RECORD.**

On his 28th birthday, Shaquille O'Neal scored **61 POINTS IN A GAME—** the most ever scored by an NBA player on their birthday.

The odds of being born on **LEAP DAY** are about **ONE IN 1,461.**

FOR ITS **100TH BIRTHDAY,** CRAYOLA MADE A 15-FOOT (4.6-M)-HIGH, 1,500-POUND (680-KG) CRAYON WITH **"LEFTOLAS,"** BITS OF OLD CRAYONS.

One type of ram, Aries's symbol, has

HORNS

that **weigh more** than all the rest of the bones in its body

put together.

Birthday cakes were a **luxury** until the **18th century,** when ingredients became more affordable.

In early 20th-century England, people sometimes had their **teeth removed** and were given **false teeth** instead for their wedding or 21st birthday.

120

To celebrate its 100th birthday, one fast-food chain offered "BIRTHDAY CAKE ON A STICK."

In several U.S. states, you can buy **cupcakes** from an **ATM.**

ACCORDING TO LEGEND, DECEMBER'S BIRTHSTONE, **TURQUOISE,** CAN BE USED AS **A LOVE CHARM.**

ROCKET SCIENTISTS CELEBRATED THE BIRTHDAY OF THEIR COMPANY'S COFOUNDER BY **FIRING A ROCKET** ENGINE TO LIGHT CANDLES ON HIS CAKE.

If a person grew at the same rate from infancy to adulthood, they'd be an average of **20 FEET** (6 m) tall by age 25.

The world's **longest** flower structure was a **dragon**

made with **112,800 pots of chrysanthemums,** November's birth flower.

The Aztec celebrated the birthday of a **GOD** with an early form of the **PIÑATA,** breaking an ornament-filled clay pot with a stick.

Capricorn's symbol is the **sea goat:** a mountain goat with a fish tail.

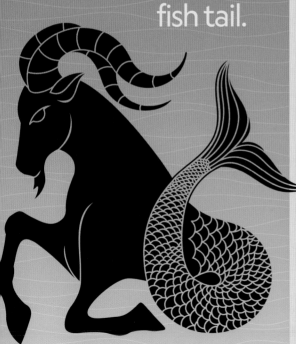

People once believed that wearing **TOPAZ,** November's birthstone, would make them smarter.

You can buy birthday-cake-scented sunscreen and an all-in-one shampoo, shower gel, and **BUBBLE BATH.**

RITUALS LIKE **BLOWING OUT CANDLES** CAN CHANGE HOW BIRTHDAY CAKE FLAVORS ARE PERCEIVED, MAKING THE CAKE **TASTE BETTER.**

You can make a cake with a **box of treats** hidden inside; add a cake topper to the box to pull out the **surprise.**

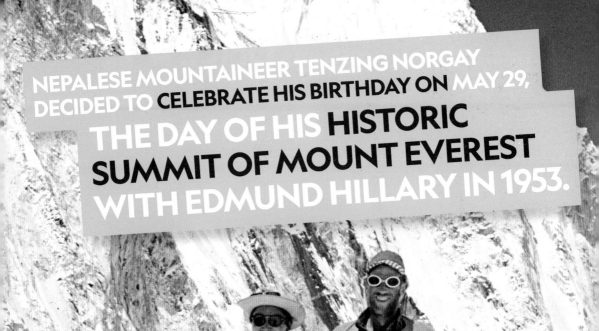

NEPALESE MOUNTAINEER TENZING NORGAY DECIDED TO CELEBRATE HIS BIRTHDAY ON MAY 29, THE DAY OF HIS HISTORIC SUMMIT OF MOUNT EVEREST WITH EDMUND HILLARY IN 1953.

Your birthday happens ONCE A YEAR—

88 EARTH DAYS
ON MERCURY

687 EARTH DAYS
ON MARS

225 EARTH DAYS
ON VENUS

TRAVEL AROUND THE SUN.
To get from one birthday to the next, it would take ...

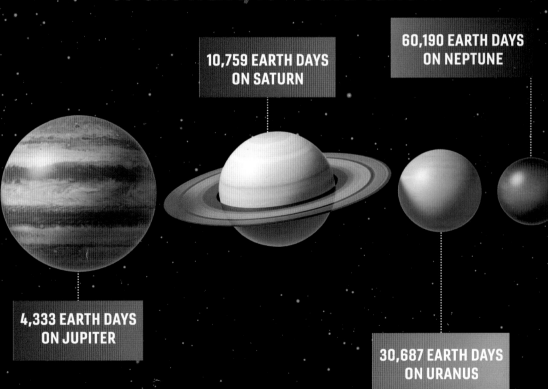

10,759 EARTH DAYS ON SATURN

60,190 EARTH DAYS ON NEPTUNE

4,333 EARTH DAYS ON JUPITER

30,687 EARTH DAYS ON URANUS

That means that a 10-YEAR-OLD on Earth would be ...

5 YEARS OLD ON MARS

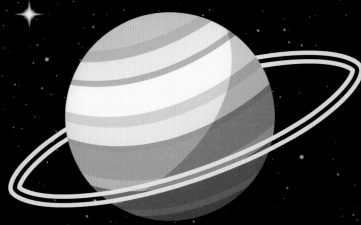

0.3 YEAR OLD ON SATURN

.06 YEAR OLD ON NEPTUNE

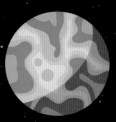

41 YEARS OLD ON MERCURY

0.8 YEAR OLD ON
JUPITER

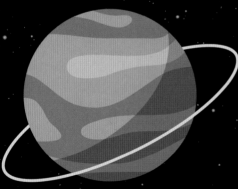

0.1 YEAR OLD ON
URANUS

16 YEARS OLD ON
VENUS

133

IF AN AMETHYST WOODSTAR HUMMINGBIRD BEGAN **FLAPPING ITS WINGS** ON YOUR BIRTHDAY AND DIDN'T STOP UNTIL THE NEXT, IT WOULD FLAP ITS WINGS AROUND **2.5 BILLION TIMES.**

In honor of the board game **MONOPOLY'S** 85th birthday, you could buy a glass game board decorated with more than **2,000 CRYSTALS.**

THERE IS SOME DEBATE ABOUT WHO WROTE THE SONG **"HAPPY BIRTHDAY TO YOU,"** AND WHEN.

Scorpions, the symbol of Scorpio, glow under black light.

In Italy, candy-coated **almonds** are a traditional gift when **babies** are born.

Confetti got its name from **Italian candy treats** made of nuts wrapped in a honey shell that were thrown at celebrations.

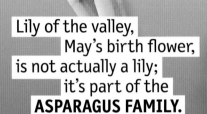

Lily of the valley, May's birth flower, is not actually a lily; it's part of the **ASPARAGUS FAMILY.**

For **KATY PERRY'S** 33rd birthday, her teacup poodle, **NUGGET,** popped out of a **CAKE.**

The record for the most birthdays spent in space is **four.**

Green-rumped parrotlets get a **"NAME"** when they're born—their parents create a particular call for them.

LEGEND HAS IT THAT THE DESIGNER OF A RAILWAY TUNNEL NEAR BATH, ENGLAND, U.K., HAD THE TUNNEL CONSTRUCTED SO THAT WHEN THE **SUN ROSE ON HIS BIRTHDAY,** LIGHT FLOODED THE BYPASS.

THE ALBUQUERQUE INTERNATIONAL
BALLOON FIESTA

BEGAN WITH 13 HOT-AIR BALLOONS

TO MARK A LOCAL RADIO STATION'S

50TH BIRTHDAY
IN 1972;

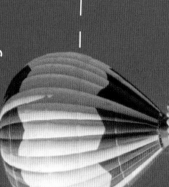

NOW MORE THAN **550 FLY** EVERY YEAR.

MIRROR-IMAGE TWINS are identical twins who have some of the same physical features, like a dimple, but on **OPPOSITE SIDES** of their bodies.

ACCORDING TO ASTROLOGICAL TRADITION, ANYONE BORN ON A WEDNESDAY IS **TALKATIVE AND LOVES TO TRAVEL,** THANKS TO THE DAY'S RULING PLANET, **MERCURY.**

One bakery makes birthday cake **"GUTS":** mashed-up birthday cake and cookies in a jar.

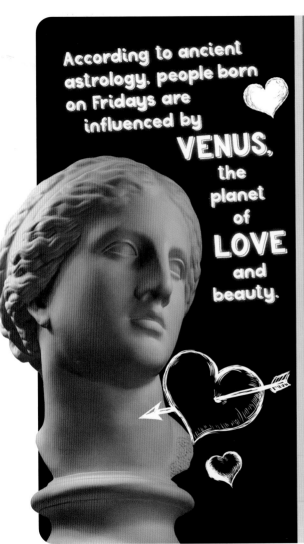

According to ancient astrology, people born on Fridays are influenced by **VENUS,** the planet of **LOVE** and beauty.

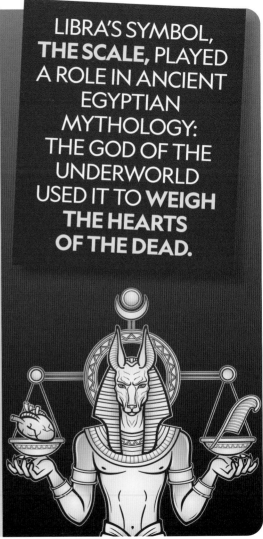

LIBRA'S SYMBOL, **THE SCALE,** PLAYED A ROLE IN ANCIENT EGYPTIAN MYTHOLOGY: THE GOD OF THE UNDERWORLD USED IT TO **WEIGH THE HEARTS OF THE DEAD.**

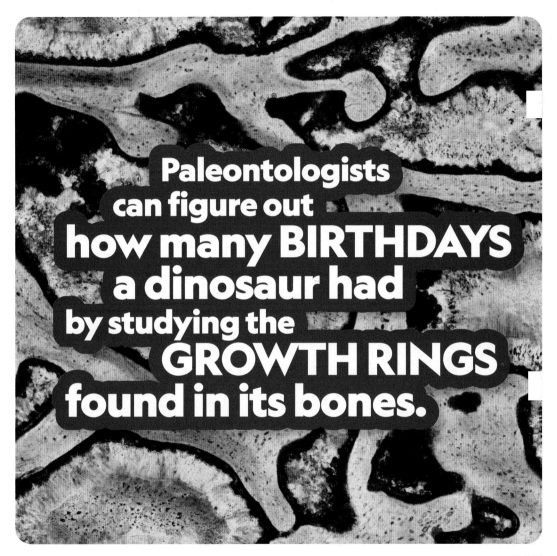

Paleontologists can figure out **how many BIRTHDAYS** a dinosaur had by studying the **GROWTH RINGS** found in its bones.

BY TRAVELING TO **DIFFERENT TIME ZONES,** ONE MAN **CELEBRATED** HIS BIRTHDAY FOR **48 HOURS STRAIGHT!**

YOU CAN HIRE A PROFESSIONAL MERMAID TO PERFORM AT YOUR BIRTHDAY PARTY.

TWO U.S. BROTHERS HAVE THE **WORLD'S LARGEST** COLLECTION OF GIFT CARDS: **3,215**

Baby

gain about

200 pounds
(90 kg)

blue whales

every day

until their first birthday.

THE OXFORD ENGLISH DICTIONARY'S **BIRTHDAY WORD GENERATOR** SHOWS USERS A WORD THAT WAS

"BORN"

IN THEIR BIRTH YEAR.

Rats, one of the animals of the Chinese zodiac, can have **up to 70 whiskers** on their faces, which they use to **explore the world.**

FROM **ONE BIRTHDAY** TO THE **NEXT** ...

YOUR **HEART WILL BEAT** MORE THAN **42 MILLION TIMES.**

YOUR **NAILS WILL GROW** ABOUT **1.2 INCHES (3 CM).**

THE **POPULATION OF THE WORLD** WILL GROW BY ABOUT **80 MILLION PEOPLE.**

The world's largest

balloon animal

ever created by one person—

a bat hanging upside down—

measured 36.8 feet (11.22 m) tall and 71.9 feet (21.91 m) wide.

Some experts think that **LIT CANDLES** first appeared on cakes in **ANCIENT GREECE** to honor the goddess **ARTEMIS.**

TO CELEBRATE THE SEVENTH BIRTHDAY OF **MR. TRASH WHEEL,** A MACHINE IN BALTIMORE, MARYLAND, U.S.A., THAT COLLECTS WASTE, THE CITY CREATED A MOSAIC ENTIRELY FROM **RECYCLED MATERIALS.**

According to the ancient practice of **numerology,** which people around the world believed to **predict the future,** people can use their birth date to find their **"life path"** number, which can reveal more about their personalities.

To **calculate your life path number,** you add up all the single digits of your birth day, month, and year, then add the digits of that number until you have a single digit.

1
People with the life path number 1 are thought to make **GREAT LEADERS.**

2
People whose life path number is 2 are thought to make **GREAT FRIENDS.**

3
The life path number 3 means that a person is thought to be **CREATIVE.**

4 People with the life path number 4 are thought to be **WISE.**

5 The life path number 5 means that a person is thought to be **ADVENTUROUS.**

6 People with the life path number 6 are thought to be **CARING** and **RESPONSIBLE.**

7 People with the life path number 7 are thought to be **QUIET** and **IMAGINATIVE.**

8 People whose life path number is 8 are thought to be **AMBITIOUS.**

9 The life path number 9 means that a person is thought to be **GENEROUS.**

155

A TALK SHOW HOST ONCE TOOK A BITE OF A **125-YEAR-OLD CAKE** THAT A GUEST HAD BROUGHT.

ACCORDING TO **ASTROLOGICAL TRADITION,** PEOPLE BORN ON SATURDAYS ARE **WISE AND HARDWORKING,** THANKS TO THE DAY'S RULING PLANET,

SATURN.

One company makes *BIRTHDAY-CAKE-FLAVORED SODA.*

IN MEDIEVAL EUROPE, DOCTORS **USED THE ZODIAC** TO **DIAGNOSE AND TREAT ILLNESSES** OF PEOPLE BORN IN THAT SIGN.

In 1987, about **300,000 PEOPLE** walked across the

GOLDEN GATE BRIDGE

to celebrate its 50th birthday, causing the arched roadway to temporarily

FLATTEN.

159

In 2020, zookeepers at an Australian zoo treated their pandas to a **pirate-themed** birthday party.

Barbie's **birthday** is March 9, 1959, the day she was introduced at the New York Toy Fair.

IN A CONTEST CELEBRATING THE 40TH BIRTHDAY OF **THE RUBIK'S CUBE,** THE WINNER **SOLVED THE TOY IN 5.9 SECONDS.**

About **40** percent of **twins** invent their own **language.**

JOHN ADAMS

believed that the United States' birthday should be celebrated on **JULY 2,** when the Continental Congress **VOTED** for independence from British rule.

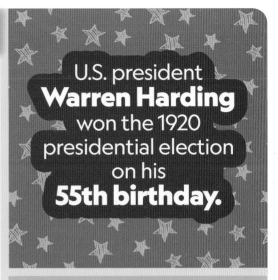

U.S. president **Warren Harding** won the 1920 presidential election on his **55th birthday.**

According to many **SUPERSTITIONS** around the world, it is **bad luck** to give scissors as a present because they might **"cut" off the friendship.**

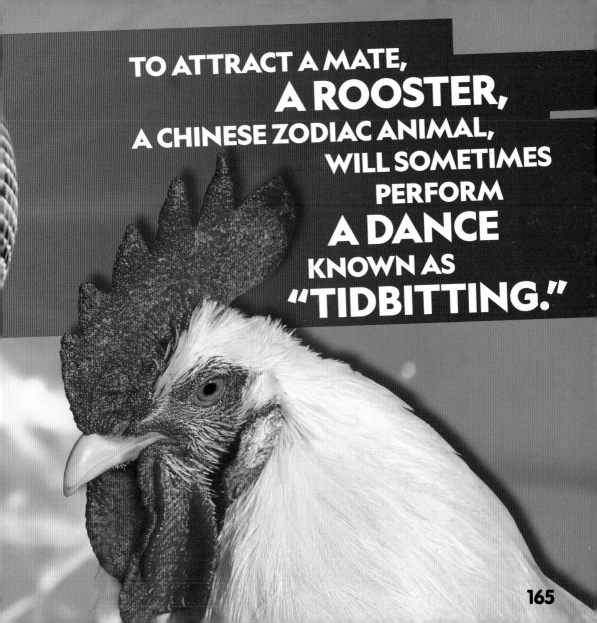

TO ATTRACT A MATE, **A ROOSTER,** A CHINESE ZODIAC ANIMAL, WILL SOMETIMES PERFORM **A DANCE** KNOWN AS **"TIDBITTING."**

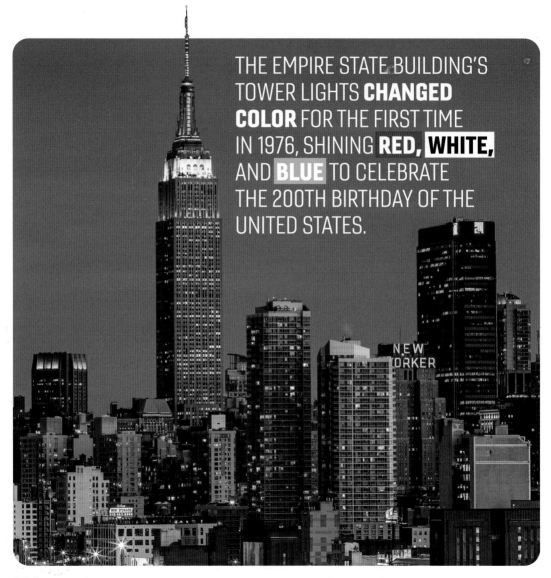

THE EMPIRE STATE BUILDING'S TOWER LIGHTS **CHANGED COLOR** FOR THE FIRST TIME IN 1976, SHINING **RED, WHITE,** AND **BLUE** TO CELEBRATE THE 200TH BIRTHDAY OF THE UNITED STATES.

NEW YORKER

THE OLDEST
BIRTHDAY
CELEBRATED
IN SPACE
WAS AN ASTRONAUT'S
60TH.

One animal
of the Chinese zodiac,
THE TIGER,
can weigh
nearly as much as
six 10-year-old kids.

Flamingos are **BORN GRAY** or white; they don't **TURN PINK** until their first or second birthday.

FAIRY BREAD— buttered bread with colorful sprinkles— is a birthday treat in Australia.

SEVERAL BAKERIES OFFER BIRTHDAY CAKES THAT LOOK LIKE **TOILET PAPER.**

PEOPLE CAN FIND OUT WHAT THE HUBBLE SPACE TELESCOPE SAW ON THE DAY AND MONTH OF THEIR BIRTH.

The Aztec likely made the first **BALLOON ANIMALS:** They twisted and inflated the dried intestines of dead animals.

The world's **oldest land animal, a giant tortoise** that lives in the Seychelles, turned **190** in 2022.

Scientists counted the rings on an **ocean quahog's shell** to discover that the clam was **507 years old,** the world's **oldest** recorded animal.

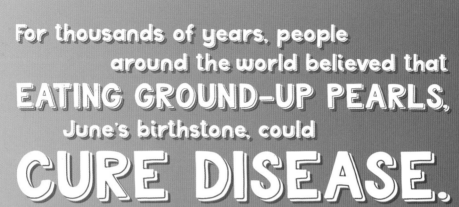

For thousands of years, people around the world believed that **EATING GROUND-UP PEARLS**, June's birthstone, could **CURE DISEASE.**

IT TOOK 20 PEOPLE MORE THAN **THREE YEARS** TO CARVE A REDWOOD TREE TRUNK INTO THE SHAPE OF A CITY-BUS-LENGTH LION, **LEO'S SYMBOL.**

IN THE "PEANUTS" COMIC STRIP, SNOOPY THE DOG ONCE HAD A BIRTHDAY CAKE WITH A **HOT DOG FOR A CANDLE.**

BASKETBALL WAS "BORN" WHEN A TEACHER INVENTED A GAME TO PLAY INSIDE DURING WINTERTIME USING **TWO PEACH BASKETS** AND A SOCCER BALL.

MORNING GLORIES,
September's birth flower, have **HEART-SHAPED LEAVES.**

ONE TYPE OF OX, A CHINESE ZODIAC ANIMAL, HAS HORNS THAT CAN SPAN ABOUT **SIX FEET** (1.8 M).

SCIENTISTS CAN TELL **HOW OLD** A GREENLAND SHARK IS BY COUNTING THE TISSUE LAYERS IN ITS **EYES.**

JUST AS SCIENTISTS GATHERED TO CELEBRATE THE **10TH BIRTHDAY** OF A VOLCANO'S FIRST ERUPTION IN CENTURIES, THE VOLCANO **BLEW ASHES** INTO THE SKY.

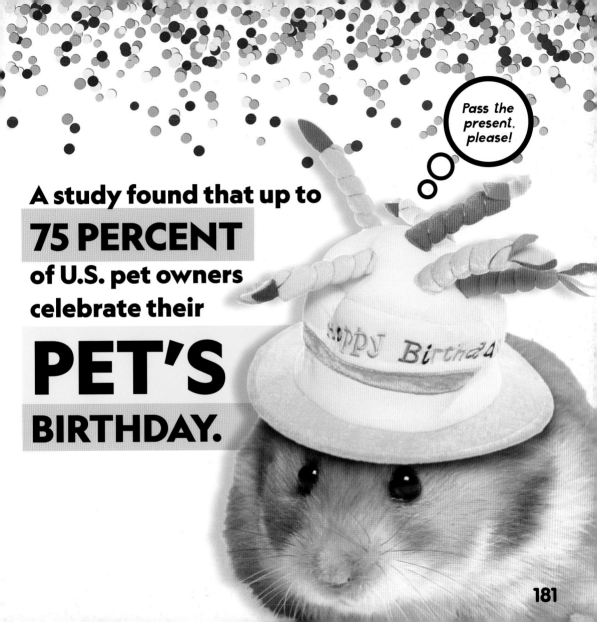

A study found that up to **75 PERCENT** of U.S. pet owners celebrate their **PET'S BIRTHDAY.**

Pass the present, please!

Scientists studied **ancient meteorites** that had fallen to Earth to determine when gas giants **Jupiter and Saturn** were **"born."**

French emperor **NAPOLEON BONAPARTE** wore **VIOLETS**, February's birth flower, in a locket around his neck because they were his wife's favorite.

A TEAM OF 34 ARTISTS MADE THE **WORLD'S LARGEST BALLOON DINOSAUR** OUT OF 150,000 BALLOONS.

People are more likely to **remember a friend's birthday** if it's close to **their own,** a study found.

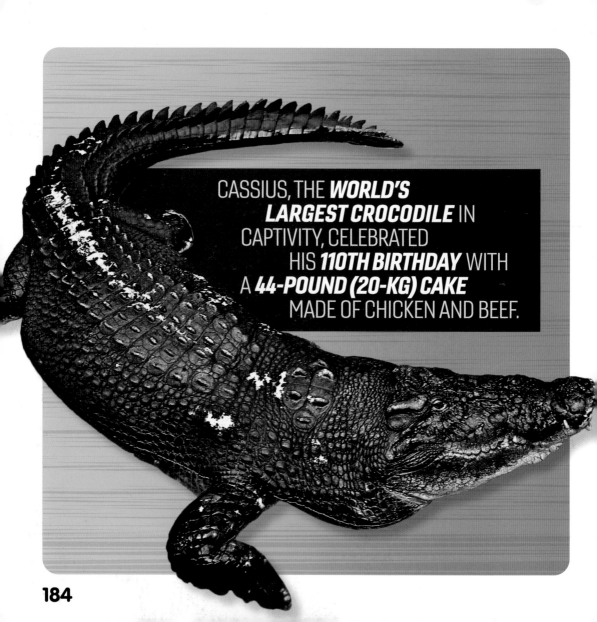

CASSIUS, THE **WORLD'S LARGEST CROCODILE** IN CAPTIVITY, CELEBRATED HIS **110TH BIRTHDAY** WITH A **44-POUND (20-KG) CAKE** MADE OF CHICKEN AND BEEF.

The world record for the most people wrapping presents at once:

1,482

You can buy **dog-friendly** cake mixes, ice cream, and party hats to celebrate your pup's birthday.

IDENTICAL TWINS HAVE **DIFFERENT FINGERPRINTS.**

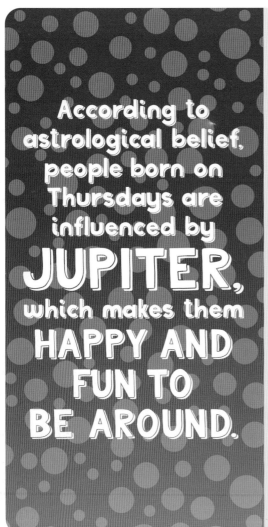

According to astrological belief, people born on Thursdays are influenced by **JUPITER,** which makes them **HAPPY AND FUN TO BE AROUND.**

For Canada's 150th birthday, the nation released the world's first circulated glow-in-the-dark coins.

A COMPANY LETS YOU **DESIGN** YOUR OWN **CONFETTI SHAPES.**

Only about **three in 1,000 births** worldwide are identical twins.

More than half of banded mongoose litters share the same birthday; being born at the same time increases their chance of survival.

In 2020, to honor U.S. president Abraham Lincoln's birthday, newborns in his hometown of Springfield, Illinois, U.S.A., received **KNITTED STOVEPIPE HATS.**

SNOWDROPS,
one of January's birth flowers,
are named after tear-shaped earrings called **"EARDROPS"**
that were popular in the 16th and 17th centuries.

In astrological legend, people born on Tuesdays have a **fiery spirit** and **lots of energy** because they are influenced by **Mars.**

IN 19TH-CENTURY EUROPE, IT BECAME TRADITIONAL TO GIVE A NEWBORN BABY A SILVER SPOON TO SYMBOLIZE **WEALTH AND HEALTH.**

THE SCIENTIFIC NAME FOR **LARKSPUR,** JULY'S BIRTH FLOWER, COMES FROM THE GREEK WORD FOR "DOLPHIN"; THE BUDS WERE THOUGHT TO RESEMBLE A **DOLPHIN'S NOSE.**

The center of the **Virgo constellation** includes a cluster of around **2,000 galaxies.**

When one Mali ruler visited Egypt in the 14th century, he **gave out so many presents** that he accidentally **lowered the value of gold.**

Did you hear that?

Scientists can tell how many birthdays a whale has had by looking at its **earwax.**

HAPPENS THE YEAR YOUR AGE MATCHES THE DAY OF YOUR BIRTH.

Boldface indicates
illustrations.

NATIONAL GEOGRAPHIC and Yellow Border Design are trademarks of the National Geographic Society, used under license.

Since 1888, the National Geographic Society has funded more than 14,000 research, conservation, education, and storytelling projects around the world. National Geographic Partners distributes a portion of the funds it receives from your purchase to National Geographic Society to support programs including the conservation of animals and their habitats. To learn more, visit natgeo.com/info.

For more information, visit nationalgeographic.com, call 1-877-873-6846, or write to the following address:

National Geographic Partners, LLC
1145 17th Street NW
Washington, DC 20036-4688 U.S.A.

For librarians and teachers: nationalgeographic.com/books/librarians-and-educators

More for kids from National Geographic: natgeokids.com

National Geographic Kids magazine inspires children to explore their world with fun yet educational articles on animals, science, nature, and more. Using fresh storytelling and amazing photography, *Nat Geo Kids* shows kids ages 6 to 14 the fascinating truth about the world—and why they should care. **natgeo.com/subscribe**

For rights or permissions inquiries, please contact National Geographic Books Subsidiary Rights: bookrights@natgeo.com

Designed by Kathryn Robbins and Shannon Pallatta

Trade paperback ISBN: 978-1-4263-7323-7
Reinforced library binding ISBN: 978-1-4263-7330-5

The publisher would like to thank Grace Hill Smith and Paige Towler, authors and researchers; Avery Naughton, project editor; Hilary Andrews and Lori Epstein, photo editors; Alix Inchausti, production editor; and Anne LeongSon and Gus Tello, associate designers.

Printed in China
22/PPS/1

PHOTO CREDITS

AD=Adobe Stock; GI=Getty Images; SS=Shutterstock

Cover: (gifts), Ivonne Wierink/AD; (dog), Ermolaev Alexandr/AD; (ribbons), Elena Barbakova/SS; Spine: (ribbons), Elena Barbakova/SS; (gifts), Ivonne Wierink/AD; Back Cover: Ljupco Smokovski/SS; Interior: 1, Elena Barbakova/SS; 2 (LE), adogslifephoto/iStockphoto/GI; 2 (RT), Ruth Black/SS; 4-5, Jenifoto/AD; 6 (UP LE), Masayoshi Matsumoto; 6 (UP LE background), Ann Sureewan/SS; 6 (UP RT), Ron Dale/SS; 6 (UP RT background), Ron Dale/SS; 6 (LO RT), playstuff/AD; 7, Anatoly Maslennikov/AD; 8, Kate Smith/SS; 9, Best dog photo/SS; 9 (paw print), Matias Giamportone/SS; 10-11, Rich Schultz/GI; 12 (UP LE), Everett/SS; 12 (UP RT), Everett/SS; 12 (LO), ULTRA.F/Stockbyte/GI; 13, Digital Storm/AD; 14 (LE), Igor Serazetdinov/AD; 14 (RT), azurita/AD; 15 (LE), Carpe Diem - Flora/Alamy Stock Photo; 15 (UP RT), Ingram; 15 (LO RT), jrbarnett/SS; 16, Andrew F. Kazmierski/SS; 17 (LE), Loree Sandler/Let them Eat Candles; 17 (UP RT), Mega Pixel/SS; 17 (LO RT), Boxyray/SS; 17 (LO background), Abe/AD; 18-19, Denis Belitsky/SS; 20 (LE), topvectors/AD; 20 (RT), Rodica Ciorba/SS; 21, Tomas Tichy/SS; 22 (UP LE), Amawasri Pakdara/SS; 22 (UP RT), 5 second Studio/SS; 22 (LO), Victoria/AD; 23, Kristian Laine/SS; 24-25, Stephen Lovekin/GI; 26 (UP), Nadia Snopek/AD; 26 (LO), Pat Sullivan/AP/SS; 27, Heiko Kiera/SS; 28 (LE), Tatiana Atamaniuk/AD; 28 (RT), Forgem/SS; 29 (LE), Rita Kochmarjova/SS; 29 (RT), Tornado design/SS; 30 (UP), thruer/AD; 30 (LO), Eric Isselee/SS; 31 (UP LE), Viachaslau Krasko/SS; 31 (UP RT), Beboy/AD; 31 (UP RT background), Alisa/AD; 31 (LO), Art of Drawing/Alamy Stock Photo; 32-33, Delpixel/SS; 32, Kristi Blokhin/SS; 34 (UP LE), Jose Ignacio Soto/SS; 34 (UP RT), vovan/SS; 34 (LO), Vilor/SS; 35, Trophy Cupcakes & Party; 35 (background), Oksancia/AD; 36 (UP), Jemastock/AD; 36 (LO), NASA/JPL-Caltech/MSSS; 37 (UP), Evgeny Dubinchuk/SS; 37 (LO), alan/AD; 38 (LE), joffin jose/SS; 38 (RT), Vladimir Zotov/SS; 38 (background), shino-b/iStockphoto; 39, Max Mumby/Indigo/AD; 40, White House Photo/Alamy Stock Photo; 41 (UP RT), All Canada Photos/Alamy Stock Photo; 41 (UP LE), nikiteev_konstantin/SS; 41 (LO), Ingram; 42 (LE), AnatoliYakovenko/iStockphoto/GI; 42 (RT), VTR/Alamy Stock Photo; 42 (background), Valeriy Kachaev/SS; 43, WaterFrame/Alamy Stock Photo; 44, Elizabeth A. Cummings/SS; 45 (UP), Valeriy Lebedev/SS; 45 (LO), JGI/Jamie Grill/Blend Images/Brand X/GI; 46 (LE), Image Source/GI; 46 (RT), Lyudmyla Kharlamova/SS; 47, JStaley401/SS; 48 (UP), U.S. Army; 48 (LO), Keith Homan/SS; 49, Marko Von Der Osten/imageBROKER/SS; 50 (LE), whitemay/Digital Vision Vectors/GI; 50 (RT), Li Ding/AD; 51 (UP), Alexander Lysenko/SS; 51 (LO), vgeny Dubinchuk/SS; 51 (background), one AND only/SS; 52 (LE), Metropolitan Museum of Art. Purchase by subscription, 1895/Metropolitan Museum of Art; 52 (UP RT), lily2014/SS; 52 (LO RT), Nikulina Tatiana/SS; 53, Margaret Norton/NBCU Photo Bank/NBCUniversal via GI; 54-55, iidea studio/SS; 55, mhatzapa/SS; 56 (UP), mdlne/SS; 56 (LO), Ben Molyneux/Alamy Stock Photo; 57, Lumenks/SS; 58, Micah Burke/AD; 59 (UP LE), lazyllama/AD; 59 (UP RT), 4LUCK/SS; 59 (LO), Ljupco Smokovski/AD; 60 (UP LE), Lightstock; 60 (UP RT), Ruth Black/SS; 60 (LO), oum/AD; 61, Eric Isselée/AD; 62, sevenke/SS; 62-63, movit/SS; 64 (UP), DalaiFood/AD; 64 (LO LE), Everett Collection/AD; 64 (LO RT), ratatosk/AD; 65, lzf/SS; 66, driftwood/AD; 67 (UP LE), Historia/SS; 67 (UP RT), kargona/AD; 67 (LO RT), Division of Political and Military History, National Museum of American History, Smithsonian Institution; 67 (background), picalotta/iStockphoto/GI; 68-69, tobkatrina/SS; 68-69 (music notes), Martial Red/SS; 70 (UP), Alexander Potapov/AD; 70 (LO LE), Sarawut Aiemsinsuk/SS; 70 (LO RT), Anne Sanders/AD; 70 (background), vector_ann/SS; 71, AP/SS; 72 (UP), jkraft5/AD; 72 (LO LE), dedMazay/SS; 72 (LO RT), H.Elvin/SS; 73 (LE), Harry How/GI/Copyright 2021 NBAE; 73 (RT), Streeter Lecka/GI; 73 (background), Axel Wolf/SS; 74, NASA's Scientific Visualization Studio; 75 (UP LE), Hurst Photo/SS; 75 (LO LE), Alisa/AD; 75 (LO RT), Jeanne-Studio/SS; 76-77, Valentin Flauraud/EPA/SS; 78, Bebeto Matthews/AP/SS; 79 (UP), Underwood Archives/UIG/SS; 79 (CTR), Limolida Design Studio/SS; 79 (LO LE), vladwel/SS; 79 (LO RT), Leung Cho Pan/Dreamstime; 80 (UP), Marcus Ingram/GI for OREO Chocolate Candy Bar; 80 (LO), Juulijs/AD; 81, Sonsedskaya/Dreamstime; 81 (background), HPL17/SS; 82-83 (UP), iuliiawhite/AD; 82-83 (LO), John Broomfield/Museums Victoria; 84 (UP LE), Milya Shaykh/SS; 84 (UP RT), stockcam/iStockphoto/GI; 84 (LO), Omer Fuat/AD; 85, Roberto Brancolini/SS; 85 (background), Valeriy Kachaev/SS; 86, Wang LiQiang/SS; 87 (UP), NASA/JPL-Caltech; 87 (LO), Darwin Wiggett/Photodisc/GI; 88 (UP), Garbage Truck Pinata

designed and sold by Kanos Toy Box, Owner, Mary Aranki. Manufactured by Aztec Imports, Inc., Owner, Al Balibrera; 88 (LO), Milano M/SS; 89 (UP RT), Lidiia/SS; 89 (CTR RT), saberstudio/SS; 89 (LO RT), yevgeniy11/SS; 89 (LE), Parinya/SS; 90-91, NASA (see individual web page for full credit); 92 (UP LE), Sharok Hatami/SS; 92 (LO LE), LoopAll/SS; 92 (RT), sportpoint/AD; 93, Julie Clopper/SS; 93 (background), aga7ta/AD; 94, Snap/SS; 95 (LE), Pavel1964/SS; 95 (RT), Nastya22/SS; 96-97, Vigoramortis/Dreamstime; 98 (LE), Renani Jewels; 98 (RT), Theo Wargo/GI; 99, Sri Chinmoy Centre; 100, arquez/SS; 101 (UP LE), Selenka/Dreamstime; 101 (LO LE), Ron Dale/SS; 101 (RT), Purchase, Gifts in memory of Mrs. Thomas Clearwater, Leo D. Bretter Gift, Bequest of Adeline R. Brown, by exchange, Osceola Foundation, Inc. Gift, and Gifts of Dr. and Mrs. A.L. Garbat, Manya Garbat/Metropolitan Museum of Art; 102, Ivan Kmit/AD; 103 (UP RT), Bryan Solomon/SS; 103 (CTR RT), pixelsnap/SS; 103 (LO RT, STILLFX/SS; 103 (LE), DragoNika/SS; 104-105, Eric Isselee/SS; 106 (UP), Hayati Kayhan/AD; 106 (LO), reptiles4all/SS; 107, Pi-Lens/SS; 108, Kiev.Victor/SS; 109, Kucher Serhii/SS; 110-111, Jean-Francois Rioux/AD; 112, Mary Durden/AD; 113 (UP), fermate/iStockphoto/GI; 113 (LO), lawcain/AD; 114, NASA; 115 (UP LE), Jakub Krechowicz/SS; 115 (UP RT), Marina Dekhnik/SS; 115 (LO), Picsfive/SS; 116, Ruth Black/AD; 117 (LE), Andrew D. Bernstein/NBAE via GI; 117 (RT), Yellow Cat/SS; 118-119, Ghost Bear Photography/AD; 120 (UP), AngiePhotos/iStockphoto/GI; 120 (LO), Saskia Massink/AD; 121, HannarongKamnim/SS; 122 (UP), melissamn/SS; 122 (LO), Ruth Black/SS; 123 (UP RT), NeMaria/SS; 123 (CTR RT), Valentina Vectors/SS; 123 (LO RT), pambudi/SS; 123 (LE), Andrea Izzotti/AD; 124-125, Imaginechina Limited/Alamy Stock Photo; 126, pixelrobot/AD; 127 (UP RT), Sudowoodo/SS; 127 (LO RT), fruitcocktail/AD; 127 (LE), KHAz/AD; 128 (UP LE), NYgraphic/SS; 128 (LO LE), Alisa/AD; 128 (RT), Farbai/AD; 129, Royal Geographical Society via GI; 130-131, AlexLMX/SS; 130-131 (background), Forgem/SS; 132-133, Golden Vector/SS; 132-133 (background), Forgem/SS; 134 (UP), Thelma/AD; 134 (LO LE), Jezper/SS; 134 (LO RT), glenncholmes/AD; 134 (LO RT background), vector_ann/SS; 135, Aleksey Stemmer/SS; 136, fusolino/AD; 137 (LE), Jiang Hongyan/SS; 137 (RT), dandesign86/AD; 138, tanapon/AD; 139 (UP), robin chittenden/Alamy Stock Photo; 139 (LO), Greater Western Limited; 140-141, Joseph Sohm/SS; 142, Mary Swift/SS; 143 (UP), Zarya Maxim/AD; 143 (LO), lilechka75/AD; 144 (LE), Ded Pixto/AD; 144 (CTR), nikiteev_konstantin/SS; 144 (RT), Zvereva Yana/SS; 145, Bernardo Cesare/Microckscopica/Science Source; 146, Potowizard/SS; 147 (LO), smile23/AD; 147 (UP), solarseven/SS; 148-149, eco2drew/iStockphoto/GI; 150 (UP), Bilevich Olga/SS; 150 (UP background), vector_ann/SS; 150 (LO), Pakhnyushchyy/Dreamstime; 151, Anton Watman/SS; 152 (UP), Rosa Jay/SS; 152 (LO), Ruslan Gilmanshin/AD; 153, Hilary Andrews; 154-155, wedelncindy/AD; 156, sumnersgraphicsinc/AD; 157 (LE), Palo_ok/SS; 157 (LE background), anna_leni/AD; 157 (UP RT background), art-sonik/SS; 158-159, Ed Perlstein/Redferns/GI; 158-159 (background), picoStudio/AD; 159 (LO LE), vector_ann/SS; 160, Morne de Klerk/GI; 160 (background), medejaja/SS; 161 (UP), Dolly MJ/SS; 161 (LO), gd_project/SS; 162, kanpisut/AD; 163 (LE), millefloreimages/AD; 163 (RT), Armin Staudt/SS; 164-165, Aksenova Natalya/SS; 164-165 (background), Evannovostro/SS; 166, mandritoiu/AD; 167 (UP), Vadim Sadovski/SS; 167 (LO), Eric Isselee/Dreamstime; 167 (background), Dzmitry Kim/SS; 168, PixilRay/AD; 169 (UP), millefloreimages/AD; 169 (LO), Mohd Rasfan/AFP via GI; 170, nerthuz/AD; 170-171, NASA, ESA, A. Goobar (Stockholm University), and the Hubble Heritage Team (STScI/AURA); 171, Lutsina Tatiana/SS; 172 (UP), Magryt/AD; 172 (LO), Steve Collender/SS; 172 (LO RT), New Africa/AD; 173 (UP), Gianluigi Guercia/AFP via GI; 173 (LO), Jiratthitikaln Maurice/SS; 174, ANCH/SS; 175 (UP), Sipa/SS; 175 (LO), Photo 12/Alamy Stock Photo; 176 (UP LE), Anastasiia Malinich/AD; 176 (LO LE), MF productions/SS; 176 (LO RT), Steve Cukrov/SS; 177, anankkml/AD; 178-179, dottedyeti/AD; 180, IndustryAndTravel/AD; 181 (UP), picoStudio/AD; 181 (LO), chrisbrignell/SS; 182 (UP), Tryfonov/AD; 183 (LO), antonel/AD; 184, Brian Cassey/EPA/SS; 185 (UP), Frog 974/AD; 185 (LO), adogslifephoto/AD; 186-187, Comaniciu Dan/SS; 188 (UP), © 2022 Royal Canadian Mint. All rights reserved.; 188 (LO), LiliGraphie/SS; 189, Kris Timken/Tetra images RF/GI; 190 (UP), Adam Jones/Danita Delimont/AD; 190 (LO), katrinaelena/AD; 190 (background), picoStudio/AD; 191, Glenn Nagel/Dreamstime; 192, NASA/SS; 193 (UP), Krakenimages/AD; 193 (LO), kostiuchenko/AD; 194 (UP), NASA/JPL-Caltech/SSC; 194 (LO), Chirawan/AD; 195, Chris/AD; 196-197, Magryt/AD; 196-197 (background), Susii/SS

JUST FOR YOU!

Keep track of all your special days, friends' birthdays, school assignments, and more in this one-of-a-kind spiral-bound planner! Every day is Funday with wacky prompts and amazing facts about the world.

NATIONAL GEOGRAPHIC KIDS

weird but true!

DAILY PLANNER

365 Days to Fill with School, Sports, Friends, and Fun!

More than 35 Weird But True books!

COLLECT THEM ALL!